# *at* GERONIMO'S GRAVE

# *at* GERONIMO'S GRAVE

## ARMAND · GARNET · RUFFO

2001

COTEAU BOOKS

Edited by Patrick Lane.

Cover photos: "Cloudscape," Mad Dog Studios; "Geronimo in Model-T,"
courtesy Library of Congress; "Portrait of Geronimo," FPG International.
Cover photo montage, cover, and book design by Duncan Campbell.

Printed and bound in Canada at AGMV Marquis.

**National Library of Canada Cataloguing in Publication Data**

Ruffo, Armand Garnet, 1955-
At Geronimo's grave

Poems.
ISBN 1-55050-176-3

1. Geronimo, 1829-1909–Poetry.
2. Indians of North America–Poetry. 1. Title.

PS8585.U514A88 2001      C811'.54      C2001-910342-5
PR9199.3.R77A88 2001

COTEAU BOOKS                    AVAILABLE IN THE US FROM
401-2206 Dewdney Ave.          General Distribution Services
Regina, Saskatchewan           4500 Witmer Industrial Estates
Canada   S4R 1H3               Niagara Falls, NY, 14305-1386

The publisher gratefully acknowledges the financial assistance of the
Saskatchewan Arts Board, the Canada Council for the Arts, the Government
of Canada through the Book Publishing Industry Development Program
(BPIDP), and the City of Regina Arts Commission, for its publishing program.

*Contents*

## AT GERONIMO'S GRAVE

## DRUM SONG

## ADDRESS UNKNOWN

## DANCE TO HOLD ON

*For my brother Anthony Wayne Ruffo, who shares in the old way,*

*and in memory of Mary (Orr) Slaney, Brian Espaniel,*
*Bill (Esher) Ritchie, and Wilfred Pelletier.*

Knowing the force and action of fire, water, air, the stars, the heavens, and all other bodies that surround it, men can be the masters and possessors of nature.
— *René Descartes (1596–1650)*

The sun, the darkness, the winds, are all listening to what we say.
— *Geronimo (1829–1909)*

*"Geronimo at the St. Louis Worlds Fair"*
*— courtesy the Smithsonian Institute.*

# *at* GERONIMO'S GRAVE

# POWER

From where does the Power
come? The old ones see it
in a moment of desert twilight,
in a basket of slithering snakes,
lumbering in a white-tipped bear,
flying in a crow that speaks,
see it in you.

Beware. Do not pray
for what you might receive.
This beast, this stallion
is not for the weak willed
who bloat like frog
for personal gain
and turn themselves
to dust.

From where does the Power
come? In the voice
that calls four times your name
when wife and children
are murdered. Tells you
no bullet will harm you
(as none ever does)
as it breathes
into you.

## CREATION STORY

Ascending we arrive at the end of the line
descend into Santa Fe, city of my longing
to see the world in a current of silver
and turquoise. Here under a portico of stone
eager tourists press, strangers to the people
who set out their blankets and rows
of jewellery in the age called America.
Here there are boutiques, galleries, churches.
I enter each and arrive to ask, how do we connect
to the sacred space between arrival
and departure? One step
and change is forever.

And I am at another place closer to who I am,
or think I am, steering straight ahead
travelling for what seems forever,
the sound of waves making me sing its rhythm.
Sixteen and dreaming of offerings of light
in the great beyond. Before I left
and met you, fell out of the sky
of my world, dove overboard,
and came up with a piece of soil
that turned into a warm body who smiled
and said I would never again
be the same.

Santa Fe, city of myth and glitter.
I hold to a company of friends
who hold hands to eyes to shield sun
and talk intimately of love and madness
in a time when power is a slogan,
a bullet, an ability to speak.
What would you say if you could see this stranger
standing in brilliant New Mexico?
This moment an amulet around my neck
I hold and stroke delicately
as though our hands were joined to the years
that amass in the burning heat,
blowing all the way back
to the creation
of us.

Fierce, tenacious, master of guerrilla warfare.

It's what the history books say. Though
at his grave, out of an unyielding sun,
and into a sanctuary of leafy shade, I move
through all that is said and not said
and touch the flowers left for him,
which make me wonder if it is possible for anyone
to have the last word. And I am reminded
that it took five thousand troops to track down
what was left of his Apache, thirty-five
men, women and children. Caught,
they say herded from New Mexico to Florida to Alabama
and finally all the way here to Oklahoma, to so-called
Indian territory (as if the rest of the country wasn't).

They say more.

That by the time he died at eighty he had embraced Christianity
and even taken part in a Presidential inauguration.
Part of the parade I suspect, the evidence committed
to memory: last year in England, at the Brighton Museum
(of all places), I bought a postcard of him lost
behind the wheel of a Model T Ford,
looking like he had just fallen out of the sky and
onto the driver's seat. Portrait of an old Chief in a top hat.
(It was my only purchase.) From there to here in one fatal swoop
as though giant talons have dropped me unexpectedly
onto this site. If I could I would ask him
if he too got plucked up by something larger than himself.

Last of the holdouts, they call him.

This morning at Fort Sill I saw the windowless cellar
they held him in (not open to the public)
and the other building they transferred him to,
the one turned into a museum and whitewashed.
A notice said he really spent little time in his cell
since he had the run of the place,
like a bed and breakfast, I am led to believe.
Yet, with wilted petals between my fingers soft as grace,
soft as old sorrow, and an even older sun overhead
guiding me beyond this arbour and back onto the highway,
I am left wondering about who he really was.
Oilfields and prairie flowers, barbed wire and distant mesas
red as a people locked behind aging vision
telling me it is the land that will have the last word.

For him whom they also call Prisoner of War.

## BISCO GRAVEYARD

I follow the old woman into the graveyard
peer over a field of weeds, at tilted stones,
rotting markers.
                    July's afternoon heat
breathless in the pitch of cicadas,
while she wears her winter coat, handkerchief
tied tightly over her head. Smiles toothless,
pointing out family (: Alex, Willy, Dolly, Mary,
                    Herbie, Danny, Alexander)
below my feet. A few b&w photographs
edged into ribbon-bound albums, a handful of stories
told by people on the verge of their own death
like this old lady who walks slowly,
talks quietly, as though to herself,
someone else.

## FISH TALE

My father tells me
of catching a northern pike so big
he had to tie a cord to his canoe
and head straight for shore.
And beach the canoe
and haul the beast up
to where he could club it with an axe.
One so big,
he had trouble getting it out
to the road.

He also tells of the time
my mother caught one
and wouldn't give up.
Rolling on the beach,
wrestling fingers to fin,
covered in sand
and slime
trying to stop it from slipping
back into the lake.

He warned her if she kept it
she would carry it herself.
She did.
Slung it over her back
and dragged it a quarter mile.
She had grown up hungry
and this was the biggest fish
she ever caught.
No way
was she going to let it go.

They were young, my parents,
though already with children
they both tried to keep
and lost.
My mother didn't know
the fish could have bit off her hand
or maybe she just didn't care
bent on bringing home food
for the ones left behind.

## FOR ALL THEIR FAILINGS

Mom's letter tracks me down
to tell me uncle Adam and
cousin Doug died last month,
only weeks apart.
Stranger things have happened I guess
but not lately. I still remember the time
Doug beat up Adam
after they had shared a bottle of goof.
We all felt a bit sad and ashamed
to see what had become of them.

And now I have to admit it's been too many years
and too many miles for me to feel anything,
except in the brief moment
when I hear Dad say,
nobody can call moose like Doug.
He can make them come to the shore and dance.
Hear Mom say, Adam phoned last night, he's still crying
over the forty dollars he's owed your father
for the last forty years. When
I recall that for all their failings
they were still family.

## FALLOUT

I never asked my auntie what she learned
in Residential School. What comes to mind
is her beading and sewing, the moccasins
she made for us, the precision.

What I don't recall are any hugs or kisses
like my European relatives lavished on us.
As though the heirs of Columbus had a special
claim to affection for those like us
caught in between.

## CONTEMPLATING SURRENDER

To you who braved
the good fight
your last horse shot
from under you
in the Arizona desert

You who did all you could
to create destruction
when all you saw
was destruction
of the old way of life

I ask here at the end
of the twentieth century
as I contemplate surrender
to you who lived
its beginning:

What did you see
  when you finally signed?
What did you hear
  when they spoke of progress?
What did you feel
  when they made their promises?
What did you mean
  when you said you understood?

Once upon a time I rode shotgun for a trickster kind of guy who thought we lived in a western, and it would always stay that way. The Lone Ranger and Tonto riding into the sunset. Both of us wanting to be the Lone Ranger. That's us in the picture he carried around in his head, six years old, leather holsters and cowboy hats. Fringed shirts and moccasins from my auntie. The two of us, into the world the same time, the same neighbourhood, and before long crawling into cars through windows, wrecks with doors wired shut, locked in as we had been from birth. Roaring down the road in one gear. Full speed come what may.

I wonder
where you are these days
last time
you were working in a distillery
and bought an empty barrel
you soaked
and let sit
later
we drank the whisky water
and got piss drunk
for old times' sake
talk about a hangover

How many times did we make it into town and finish up at the Sportsman's Hotel on some Friday evening. Meeting the folks from up and down the line who would come in and get loosened up. Until we too got bent out of shape and then back into the car and back into the bush. Thought we could live like that forever. Though I remember looking around at all the boozed-up old-timers and swearing their end wouldn't be mine. Some weren't even old. Like Terry. When the doctors opened him up to stop the hemorrhaging, they took one look and closed him back up again. His stomach looked like a tire blown to hell from all the Aqua Velva and cleaning fluid.

Last time we rode together
you ended up with a woman
you picked up
hitchhiking
you always
had a way with women
about the time
I decided
enough was enough
it was time
to move on
about the time
you lost your son.

Remember? We weren't much older than him when we got stuck between those two fence posts. We'd been raiding gardens for strawberries, your own mother's, which always seemed so absurd because she gave us all we wanted, but I guess you preferred to eat them at night with the earth still clinging. Or was it sitting in front of her with a blank face when she complained about the little devils. We were heading down the lane when a car appeared, and we dashed for a gateway and got jammed together. Like so much that came later, we had to wiggle our way out of that one. Like the time you ran away from home because you had fallen in lust with a girl up the line and were bound to get to her. And me walking the tracks behind you wishing I were fishing. Why I tagged along I still don't know. Though I suppose for the ride. Always the ride, and a wild one it was, riding high in trickster style.

## FAR AWAY HILLS I SEE

In the hospital's fluorescent lighting
where everything looks too white
and too clean, I encourage her.
And so she props herself up on a pillow,
pauses as though to catch a phrase,
clears her throat,
and recites her poem for me
and laughs her little laugh
after each stanza.

I tell her I love the word "whilst."
For grandma poetry is Pauline Johnson
in her buckskin
and bear-claw costume
singing the old glories of her people,
a country of canoes and traplines,
rolling hills of thick treed shadow,
and stars so bright
they hurt your eyes to look at them.

I scramble to jot down what she says,
because her poem is from the heart.
She used to talk about writing a book
but knows it will never happen.
And I wonder if it has anything to do with
the things she doesn't say.
Her first man.
Her second.
Her third. The men who left her
with children.

## BIRTH DAY POEM

Last night I spun you across the floor
and you smiled in surprise and complimented me
and I told you of a time when she
would lead me across the kitchen,
my head barely past her waist
as I counted out one, two three.
All young men should know how to dance,
young women just love to dance,
she said, waiting on the next record
(by one of the Hanks or the Strausses)
to spin the gramophone into life.

Five o'clock in the morning,
living room littered and empty,
I think of those times with my mother
who no longer dances as she once did
as a young woman, but whose voice
is still here inside me, younger
than I am today. I think of this
now, my hand pressed into hers,
my step in time with hers,
I who stand partnerless
at the window waiting
on the sun to dance
the earth into light.

## TODAY THE LAKE (AGAIN)

You move soundlessly slipping into your boots while everyone
else continues to sleep through dawn's half-light. And I whisper
across the cold cabin floor. Then we are out on the water, mist
rising like a dream over the bright lilies. And somewhere a loon,
while behind us a breeze creaking through the trees
like old bones.

For now, the two of us in silence

Unlike the night before, when we drank wine and called cards
and marked points with a blunt pencil on a yellow pad. When
I strummed an old tune about trains going on forever. And loss.
When it moves up inside us, not like wine that leaves you light-
headed and dry, but like spring water so clear you hardly notice
you're drinking. What does good water taste like anyway?

And today

I am so full from drinking that water longer than I ever thought
possible. Like that morning when the fish were jumping around
the boat, and we laughed in our frustration and said we should
just dip net them rather than try to catch them on a line. Because
the hour has turned into days and the fish are still not biting,
which has turned into weeks, and still no fish, turns into months,
and still none, which turns into years and more years. And here
I am still holding onto that thin filament, the dusty lure on my
desk.

## BIRTH OF THE SACRED

this telling a collective journey,
a path back
to a mountain with stone eyes,
this seed of beginnings
speaks of creation,
an eagle chief
dividing the darkness
into birth
   destruction
in a dragon breath,
giant arrows,
challenging a boy who is not a boy
more than himself,
   a people
as the story is more
than itself,
a guide to remembering.

# PAINLESS

By then you are living in Calgary riding horses and line dancing.
Your laughter and aching muscles everything. This before
they discovered the tumour behind your eyes, shifting
your sight upward past ceiling into prairie sky.
You who had already felt the knife at your throat.
(I helped you cover the scar
with a silk scarf from Paris.)

You who decided your job at the brokers' was no place
to spend your last days. And took what time they gave you
and gave it your best run.

Like when you were bucked black and blue and got right back on,
or else you'd never ride again, you said. Living it up
as though reaching for the tip of the snow mountains themselves,
you did what you could to keep going,
cleaned stables, stores, anything,
as long as it didn't interfere with life.
Even flirted with the thought of marrying again.

My last day there, you bought a wig for your bald chemo head,
red, the colour of your people,
your flaming arrow heart.

When you came to see me in the east, your time was up,
and we wheeled you out on the town, where you smoked pot
for medicinal purposes, and drank a beer for pleasure.
Half Irish, you loved the music and told me of searching for a father
you never knew but wanted to be buried beside.
The ache that never healed. And with the band singing
"Danny Boy" and light sliding in from the street
as if some almighty hand were holding you gently,
I wished we could have stayed that way forever.

But last call came, along with the call three days later,
you dead in your sleep, after cake with friends.
And me, thankful to hear it.

# Peepeegizaence

This January morning and the eye of the hawk
upon me, perched on the back fence,
framed by the willow arbour,
swivelling its head side to side,
waiting.

For me, oblivious to nearly everything,
stepping from the house into this special day,
while the world moves on,
a new millennium
holding out its promise.

Stopped in mid stride, like the morning,
I freeze, gasp, my breath caught
in the cold. I stare
and minutes pass,
as she scans me
and the horizon beyond.

And I know today, on my birth
day, I have a visitor who wishes me well.
When is a hawk
not a hawk? This, as she swoops
to the ground behind the fence,
and I hurry
to find her gone.

## PRAYER

I placed a braid of sweetgrass
on your coffin and sat quietly
listening to your goodbye.
Outside the sky was dark,
and I wore dark glasses
because it was still too bright.

At the graveyard the priest blessed
your passing. An Anishinabe elder
appeared, laid down tobacco
and spoke in your language.
Someone asked me who he was
and I answered a part of your life
beyond ours.

You said you wanted a feast
for all your family and friends.
My heart split and I dug my fork
deep into it and chewed
and chewed unable to let go.
The old people held my hand
and told me stories about you
as I prayed for rain.

## She Asked Me

Here we go again, Vancouver, Calgary, Ottawa,
northern Ontario, southern BC. That's what happens
when you're homeless like my grandmother said years ago
in Toronto, on Spadina Street, where she had taken refuge.

A Stranger in her Native land, she wrote in a poem,
and I agreed and brought her more tea.

Into a dream I awake, and the telephone gathers me up
in its ring. A woman's voice asks when I'm coming home,
our conversation suspended in a breath, a pattern of blue light.
Home? Her mourning song fills me with sorrow
for all we've done, from stomping out a tobacco
butt, to stomping out a life, all that has turned her sons
and daughters into strangers.

And again I awake to find myself packing to leave.

The room is a scatter of suitcases. Yesterday
(or was it the day before?) I flew through smog
and landed in San Francisco and could barely breathe.
Today the Okanagan sky is fresh with wind. Tomorrow
is where an old lady sits staring at a wall.

The end of this journey somewhere just beyond her.

Earlier, in New Mexico when the year was young,
I travelled to Gran Quivira, a sacred place, and prayed
and a whirlwind appeared like an answer. That prayer
was for you, for all of us lost to this century
turned highway.

## Rockin' Chair Lady

Today's the day I wake up knowing I'm going to commit myself
to the memory of Mildred Bailey. To my young mother
spinning her unfashionable and unpardonable jazzy 78's
(in the land of Country & Western)
on her rigged-up gramophone. Music
I couldn't appreciate, let alone understand.

These days an old woman I met out west years ago
sends me tapes from her collection
spanning seventy years. The last one of Bix Beiderbecke,
the white cornet player from the 1920s
(they say he sounded like a girl saying yes)
who played black and died at twenty-eight. Bootlegged
booze and passion will do that.

As for Mildred, the encyclopedia says
she was "The first white singer to absorb
and master the jazz-flavored phrasing, enunciation,
embellishments, improvisatory fervor,
and swinging rhythm of her black contemporaries."
To put it plainly, "the first non-black woman
to sing jazz convincingly."

What they don't say is that she was Indian,
Coeur d'Alene to be exact,
and could party with the best of them.
In jazz things are either black or white.
Red doesn't count. Unless your name is
Red Norvo, the musician Mildred lived with
for twelve years, before she got too fat and too sick.
Diabetes (the Indian disease) and heart trouble,
or trouble of the heart, claimed her in '51,
before I was even born.

But back to Mildred's young life. Bound for the city,
she got a job with the Paul Whiteman Orchestra
(talk about ironic) and hit the jazz scene
big time, in a world of big band swing.
They called her the Rockin' Chair Lady
because she was one great swinger
who sang with the greats, Goodman,
                              Dorsey,
                              Hodges,
                              Hawkins, to name a few,
and took over the airwaves on her own national show.

Imagine tuning into her voice
on your Motorola. Hot stuff in 1933.
Imagine being labelled Indian back then
and not wanting to be, because red is out,
it doesn't count,
and hearing Mildred
coming in strong, knowing she's in
all the way to the top.

*"Geronimo as a Young Warrior Holding a Rifle"*
*— courtesy the Arizona Historical Society, Tuscon*

# DRUM SONG

# NOW THAT THE GALLEONS HAVE LANDED

*Unless serious action is taken few Indigenous*
*languages to Canada will survive in the 21st century.*
— The Royal Commission on Aboriginal Peoples

Where are the words
of Turtle Island?
rooted in earth
painted on stone
and bark,
carved
into cedar
totems,
a thousand-year-old
memory

What is left
but dream
new words
in the smoke
prayer
in the angry
loss
in the weak
catch
emptied
and flailing.

What is left
but to struggle
with mouth
hooked
and discover
this tongue
fitted perfectly
is the sound

of a prisoner
on a boat
bound
to wailing
death

For the ancestors
huddled before
the story of fire,
Nanabush
his laughter
spilling
like his seed
blooming
into the tikinagan,
a baby
who sings
every syllable
of her mother
earth

This loss
my burden
as I gasp
to stay the course
in this language
shoved into
my relations
and now gathered
in my own
bundle
in my own
voice
to deafen me.

## PROMISES

You said it was the same
everywhere
and rolled up your sleeve,
and I saw what I thought was a bracelet
tattooed to skin
but was really camouflage
for a white scar
so faint it showed more the dream of death
than the actual attempt.

Call it consequence or memory.

Do you think it was any different
anywhere else?
Australia, Africa, Asia... Ireland, Scotland...
you said, when I complained
about what happened
on Great Turtle Island.
(By this time you were looking quite bored
with me, or was it sadness I detected?)

The history of the world
in one short line.
The colonizer writes the history,
        pins the medals
        takes the bows,
        names the buildings,
        cities, provinces
        whole countries.
There you have it.
But they made Treaties, I said.
Promises?
That was when you laughed.

## In the Sierra Blanca

Geronimo sits on a cloud
heavy with rain
for the cactoid earth,
catches a shaft of light
and slides with weariness
down to the land
he was forced to flee.

Geronimo walks and thinks,
kicks a rusty can
lying at the roadside,
wonders if the assassins
still gallop to the dictate,
the only good Indian
is a dead one.

He remembers when they treated
his people to a gift
of piñon nuts
seasoned with strychnine,
remembers
   (this chemical warfare)
and grimaces
an old hate.

But now there are rumours
things have got even worse.
This he finds unbelievable.
How can it be so?
He's heard they are now poisoning
the earth
mother herself.

Nuclear dump site. Low level waste
containment. State-of-the-art
concrete canisters.
English! he shakes his head
and sees a rattler
sunning itself,
forked tongue
flicking the air.

But Geronimo understands
what this is really about,
because after his surrender,
he was invited to the 1904 World's Fair,
where he sold his photograph for 25¢
and his autograph for 10¢.
Some asked to buy his buttons
and talked investment,
profit.

He smiles in this knowledge.
He had learned much
about white people. Learned
what was important to them.
But this new thing,
as though the assassins were back
or had never left,
he has to see
for himself.

# I TRIED ESCAPE

*I shall call the whole, consisting of language and the actions
into which it is woven, the "language-game."* — *Ludwig Wittgenstein*

Yesterday I tried escape,
lifted a book
that told me words are a puzzle,
an elaborate game,
offering reprieve in a geometry of distance
that sees Wittgenstein dancing
with Gertrude Stein
(Mozart, E-flat Major, K.365, Rondeaux: Allegro),
fit the pieces and win the award.

Today I visit an Anishinabe brother in jail,
and I'm reminded we are less
than five percent of the population
and make up some seventy-five percent of the prisons.
The radio mentions an eleven-year-old Innu boy
burned alive
when the gas he was sniffing
caught fire.

I am still struggling with puzzles,
the unsolvable kind,
where the award is life,
where we are bound to one endless knot,
the rope around Riel's neck
around your neck,
around my hands,
each time I try to write a poem
that offers escape.

# RAINING ICE

I live in a world of possibility where
power reigns in a bird beating on a tin can.
Dinnertime. Dreamtime.
In a solitary note, I pick out and chant to the dawn.
A simple act of defiance beyond the shadow
of the chickens that ran around my childhood
headless, going everywhere and
nowhere.

I live in a world that tells me to forget.
Just do it, the slogan of the day.
Leaving a bank fashioned into a temple,
I give a homeless man a few dollars and wonder
if he can't find work or has simply given up.
Either way, he is not alone,
an army is marching the four corners,
cold and hungry.

I listen for icebergs sliding into the ocean
as the climate warns us,
setting the stage for the next deep freeze.
I hear it signalled in the pitch
of a bird banging its last song,
in all the headless running,
in all the meaningless words,
seducing us to forget,
in a sheet of ice-rain
tearing down trees
turned into power lines.

This morning the shapes of trees swing me past Voltaire's house
where I stoop to pick a pine cone, look up at the huge windows,
heavy doors, remind myself tomorrow I'll visit the museum inside.
Much too interested in just thinking of his old enlightened words:
> All humans are formed by their age
> and very few
> rise above it.

This is Geneva, and I am on my way to search the newspapers
for something on what they are calling the "Oka Crisis."
There's not much. Two short columns. It won't last long.
(A little affair on a world scale.) The army has been called
to quell the terrorist Mohawk warriors.

Back home in the Peaceable Kingdom.

There was a time when Voltaire called Canada nothing but snow
and ice, tried to dissuade the French from such a foolish
adventure. Makes me wonder what he was really trying to tell them?
Perhaps if they believed it was worthless they might leave well enough
alone. Nothing but speculation. The one certainty
the fact of families protecting their heritage, their land.
> (During the standoff, the army shrouded the area
> in barbed wire in case the Mohawks tried to flee,
> unable to comprehend they weren't going
> anywhere.)

And the power of a pine cone in the palm of my hand. The tree
of peace, rooted in earth extending to sky, a sacred connection,
the Mohawk people.

## BABY BLUES

For the longest time we acted like we didn't know any better.

> Whether we want to or not,
> we hold ourselves up to the day
> like a glass bowl
> to see through,
> handle carefully,
> and share
> a simple orange.

But it's changed now that we can't drink the water.

> You tell me of raising your child
> on welfare,
> trying to make ends meet
> when they are frayed short,
> and smile when you mention
> his name.

Now that our diet includes ten pounds of pesticide a year.

> I tell you of sitting twenty-two floors up
> in my office perch
> over a river,
> wondering about its origin
> and where it
> will all end.

Now that the cows are brain dead, a whale is toxic waste.

> And I admit I am saddened
> (even though I try for the bright side)
> thinking of your child,
> the life stolen
> from all the children
> of the world.

As we continue to talk and chew and spin through the universe.

# I Heard Them, I Was There

*Writing in 1747 about captives, Cadwallader Colden records, 'No Arguments, no Intreaties, nor Tears of their Friends and Relations, could persuade many of them to leave their own Indian Friends and Acquaintance(s).*
— *Quoted by James Axtell in* The White Indians of Colonial America

We came in droves, by wagon, by train, by boat,
womanless, ready for anything, but wanting wealth.
I was there. I saw how we howled at an empty sky,
called upon heaven to open in a beacon of rainbow
and lead us to that ever blessed vein of gold. Yes,
I remember how we toiled with bare hands, plunged
into the bosom of earth until we tore our own flesh,
split ourselves wide open like the very land we preyed upon.
It got so that we no longer even felt, we mastered the art,
and merely stuffed our pain (and memory) into our mouths
and swallowed. Nobody ever let out a cry or whimper.
You could say we had moved into the level of sweat.

If we had faith it was in ourselves, in our backs,
our deadened minds, forged in darkness and dream.
Our God, our accomplice, always radiant and forgiving,
left us to our own devices. At night we dreamed
golden meadows, caterpillars turning to butterflies,
storms to rainbows. Some even dreamed cities,
saloons and whisky, women and sex. What else?
We all dreamed of singing, "Those were the days my friend,
we thought they'd never end," relaxing in a hot tub
with a cigar in mouth and glass in hand, and of course
with the mandatory young thing scrubbing our backs.
It's no lie. I swear. I was there in flesh and spirit.

Of course there were the other dreams. And we cursed
those who had planted them for us. I put a bottle to my lips
and found it filled with scorpions, black beetles and lice.
I threw down a hammer that squirmed into a serpent.
I awoke one night to find the bunkhouse smeared
with shit and blood. But all that, I must say, was before
a few of us dared go deep into the forest for fresh meat.
I could tell from the start that day was ripe with omen.
Away from the pit I could hear my name stirring
in the wind, could taste the fear burn in my gut, hover
in the trees, appear in the beat of crow wings
(which made us all laugh nervously).
And then, a small red sack with a braid of something
left on a rock. We burned it, damned it devil worship.

But me. I couldn't get it out of my head
and found myself labouring over it
when I should have had my mind on my work.
When I looked at my hands I saw for the first time
they were claws. My mouth stank of decay.
What did it mean this offering? Was it a message?
I went back. The rest is history. Sometimes
I still return to the edge of the clearing and watch
with eyes that see through darkness. Nothing has changed.
And I wonder what it is I am looking for sitting here
in the shivering cold. Sometimes even they ask me
as though if I explain it to them I will explain it to myself,
but I repeat I don't know. What I do know is
it has something to do with death and darkness,
disease and dream. Something to do with me
looking back at myself

## ON THE LINE

Sign, sign,
on the dotted line
and you will be mine
forever and ever,
like the mountains
and the lakes,
sky, soil,
everything I take.

I will supply you
with all
your needs,
a bible,
a blanket,
rations and beads.

If you can't understand me
don't worry
or whine,
heed what I say,
what is yours
is mine.

So sign on the line,
what more
can be said,
my word is law,
you have nothing
to dread.

You can't resist
so don't
even try,
I have cannons

and armies,
cities
and spies.

Oh, yes,
I do have a home,
it is far
far away,
but I like what I see,
and I've decided
to stay.

## GERONIMO IN BATTLE

Wounded: shot
in the right leg above the knee,
still carrying the bullet,
stabbed with a sabre
in the right leg
below the knee,
hit on top of the head
with a rifle butt,
shot through the left forearm,
shot just below the outer corner
of the left eye, shot
in the back.

But never killed,
though he killed
many. How many,
he doesn't know
because (in his words)
some weren't worth
counting. They
were always treacherous
and malicious.

## POWWOWS AND INDIANS

*Powwows are nothing more than entertainment for white people.*
*— Macleans Magazine.*

At the powwow
the old Cree
men and women
sit in a circle
of lawnchairs.
Not far away
the ruins of
the residential school
where most lost
their language,
and nearly
everything else.

For the longest
time most wouldn't
even admit
they were Indian.
(Scottish or French
the flavour of
the times.)
Not their own
doing, but drummed
into them
by the clergy.

Here the drumming
is different.
Finally.
They can be
who they are,
or at least
come to terms
with who they are.
The dark days
of forgetting
reborn in
the dancing
children.

The glow is unmistakably red.
It could be dawn,
it could be dusk,
sunrise or sunset.
It matters little. Paintings
like this are dramatic by nature,
and red is the colour of character.

His head is shaved and painted
(you guessed it: red).
Eyes steely, reptilian.
(after all this is a portrait).
Mouth severe, jaw rigid metal
(certainly wordless)
like his scalping knife.

The woman he is holding
by one white porcelain arm
has aptly swooned.
Her dress is in slight disarray
though not provocative by any stretch
of imagination.
(That is for another day.)
Fear glistens her brow.

Her face is fixed on a distant nimbus:
could it be, yes, it is,
a horse and rider,
under the cover of cloud,
her protectorate,
her angel of mercy,
brandishing sword and pistol,
thundering down with all the bravado
of legend.

This is no pastoral scene.
No English cottage country.
No Lake Windermere languidly rolling by.
No sheep lulling in the background.
This is America 1607.
The message is clear.
It is a popular pose.

## APACHE SON

Later sweating
under the weight of ink,
I think of Carl who had a hand
in this, writing poems full
of fists. On his way to the boxing club,
stopping me in the street to convince me
we must prepare to defend ourselves.

Carl speaking of his Apache ancestors,
in the streams, the air, the ground
below his very feet.
Seeing their bodies pounded
with piledrivers,
buried under concrete
used as a dump.
       Fight to save them.
       Save ourselves.
The elegant tactics of Goyathlay
remembered in this ode
to resistance.

## NEW MEXICO THEN

*A few nuggets or a small poke of dust panned from some icy stream spawned hell-roaring camps... overnight.* — The Mining Advance into the Inland Empire, *W.J. Trimble*

Always the land, always the wagonloads
coming to suck the open wound,
the veins of gold, silver, copper, iron.
The miners smell it like a horse smells water,
sights set on Indian territory,
Mimbreno's country,
arrive in a stampeding herd
to stake it with blood
(even if it's their own).

Here the law is a six-shooter.
Pepper and turpentine fortify firewater,
and women who don't wash
ply their naked trade to stay alive.
Here Indians stagger
to death's dance,
one of their scalps fetching
up to one hundred dollars
(women and children fifty).

What to do? when the Army itself
cannot (or will not) do anything.
When the shooting, stabbing,
clubbing, beating,
burns worse
than the worst whisky,
sparing no one,
not even you
who live to tell.

The child beside me is in awe at the display case:
carved tomahawks
   spiked warclubs
      silver medals.
I can see nobody ever taught him
that Indians fought alongside the British
to save his Canada from the Americans
in the War of 1812. That if not for Indians
there would be no Canada.

Once so useful, Chiefs and leaders given King George medals
for their contributions and loyalty to the Crown.

There is a story of a Chief who rallied his warriors to fight
alongside the great Shawnee Tecumseh. A photograph
of his medal worn by his grandson during the Treaty
negotiations of 1906 sits on my mantle. Taken
at the time when the land was already gone,
taken like his image, everything
up for grabs, like the medal
gone for a bag of beans,
a few drinks.

# Iron Angel

Two a.m., and the angel of death
and American myth comes riding
over the high plains,
handsome,
        nameless,
                insane,
the steely-eyed killer dismounts
dust like a halo rising above his head
as he saunters towards his prey,
another dirty cowboy
no less deadly
just uglier.

I'm in the middle of this showdown
when I find myself thinking about the holdup
in the US Congress
by the American National Rifle Assocation
which fears even a minimal restriction
on the sale of a handgun
because it infringes on the right to bear arms,
to fight the good fight,
to ride free
on wings of iron.

All this right here in my living room
in dead colour,
and me lying on the sofa
also armed,
with a quick-draw channel changer,
ready to click this assassin
into TV oblivion
the moment some Hollywood Indian
comes hollering
out of the horizon.

I write words like justice, obligation,
responsibility, treaty, suicide.
And shout them from the rooftop.
My neighbours who are in their garden,
look up and conveniently ignore me.
They think I'm drunk,
but I haven't touched a drop.
The bottle I'm holding
is actually a homemade bomb,
a poetry bomb,
that will soon shower
the sky with words
they can no longer ignore.

In the archives, another photograph of a treaty expedition, more white collars and Union Jacks. Even on this spring day, the old air of officialdom pervades, dry as August's dead heat. The commissioners dominate the page (their faith and loyalty to king and country holding them steadfast), flanked by military men, equally stiff and formal, as though on guard. For what? For who? For you, grandfather? In case you caught on to what was actually going on, what they were actually up to and tried to stop them, did something foolish — as they would say. But, no, that was never the case. By now, it is a matter of survival: with the land cut and mined, the animals gone, immigrants pouring in by the trainload, your people sick and dying.

If this bottle bomb
explodes
word shrapnel
flying every which way
responsibility hitting them between the eyes
obligation falling at their feet
justice sticking to their skin
treaty hitting them squarely
and perhaps even a word like suicide
hitting home
What would they say?
Would they find the words?

I imagine a drum beating, an old drum of worn hide with faint markings of red ochre, the power of another world. The commissioners do not notice this, instead they look at you, your people, and see a life of rags and empty bellies. They complain they don't understand all the noise, all the fuss, complain there are no real Indians left anyway. They say you are merely mimicking something you no longer understand, no longer have words for. There is a moment when they turn to the drummers and wonder when it will all end, wonder when you will finally become Canadians. Not like them, but Canadians nonetheless. In their eyes, you are like children, dependent upon the Queen mother to take care of you.

It gets to the point
where they can no longer ignore me
packing the bomb takes time
my muttering gets to them
but instead of paying attention
to what I'm saying
they run away
and dial 911
say there's a crazy man on his roof
threatening to jump
later they will tell me
they did it for my own good.

This is how I see it. From my vantage point, here in this white room, where I sit on top of a mountain of time looking down with the sight of a great eagle. The documents guaranteed health care after plagues were introduced, an education for the children, who were shipped away to residential schools where assimilation was force-fed like the mush they had to eat. But we know this, and we are told there is no use in crying over the past, because the past is today and tomorrow. Past, present and future, a life dipped into and barely held together by an old drum that I can hear even now, way up here on my perch, if I quiet myself and listen hard enough.

## THE DREAM

Trees sickly barren
under the oven sun
but for the corpses
swinging in the scorched wind
where flies lay
their maggot songs.

So bright eyes picked clean
by vultures slurping
the body's last memory.
Riders who smile
a flash of teeth
and sabre.

The dream of blood is a dream of escape into the Gila,
Mogollon, Little Burro, Santa Catalina, Guadalupe,
Chiricahua mountains, into a homeland you know
like the wet flesh in your hand.

*Suicide in Canada among Native people between the ages of 12 to 25 is the highest in the world.* — The Royal Commission on Aboriginal People.

We the wounded, shot by accident, a hunting accident,
a grand expedition so big it changed the face of the world,
our face, our world,
in which we the people ran through forests
that dead-ended
into railroads and gold mines,
as our breath pumped through us
as our power drained from us
and someone shouted Oil!
and another shouted Blood!
Caught. That's it,
no escape on an island only so big.
Turtle Island.

And wounded, that's us too, the walking wounded.
Here I am now leaning against a chair
in front of a chalkboard trying to explain,
pointing with my stump
to the light so that it's clear
where I'm limping from,
to the one with the eye gouged out
who is saying Yes, yes, I see.
As another stands to dance
almost believing she's in a birthing room
getting her parts repaired before the hole spills out
all she has managed to save of herself,
while the one over there with eyes of black water
sits and stares, hand up, calling for help
but sinking all the same,
eyes pulled back by an anchor
no less than memory's hard fuck.

And him in the corner with a zipper for a mouth,
a pocked face expressing his bluntness and rage.
Beside another so filled with sorrow
it's burnt into his wrists. And her
and him and him and her with a mind twisted
like a corkscrew,
another accident of birth.
Lips red as Cupid's cock,
red as the stuff we slurped
from brown paper bags,
in our vain attempt to forget,
in her attempt to be glossy as a magazine
so she'll be liked
like they said she would be.

Oh sister! Oh brother! You
still clenched and weeping
for your dead brother and sister,
mother and father
who shot themselves
after drinking and sniffing themselves mad
because they thought they had lost faith
in our ability to heal
our earth, heal
ourselves.
Take this wound of generations
(listen to my rib cage crack, feel my beating heart)
and wrap it in cedar and sage,
sweetgrass and tobacco,
in the medicine of our people,
wrap it in dawn
so that we might all dance east,
again.

*"Geronimo in Melon Patch at Fort Sill"*
*— courtesy the Fort Sill Museum*

# ADDRESS UNKNOWN

# LEGEND

So the legend goes Geronimo dreamed
himself into a man
with the power of horses.
In a night when the desert closed
her eyes to conceal him,
and horses,
swift and sure-footed,
carried him and his love.

To win his daughter, her father
told Geronimo to steal into an enemy camp
and bring back four horses.
Geronimo in turn proposed four times four.
Sixteen years old, he returned with twelve
and was given four
by his own people. The gesture
matching the deed.

The way she tells it with hope
in her own dark eyes, this modern
woman in this crowded room.
Talking of courage and kindness,
of falling in love the way a woman might,
if she were young enough,
or lived herself a life of starlight
with a man who would risk
everything.

There was a song I sang when we met, a old song I had learned at the kitchen table. I couldn't have been much more than ten and she would come by in the afternoon with a bottle of Golden Wedding and light sinking into her eyes, flaming across her dark face, swelling her shrunken heart. The song had to do with ships though we lived nowhere near the sea. Instead we would look past the torn blinds to the tips of a river of trees and imagine the wind as waves. All we had to do was climb aboard and sail away. The music didn't come easily, my little fingers strained through the chords, trying to make sense of the dissected sound. But the afternoons were long, and eternity, which would end only when the Golden Wedding was finished, and her magical fingers turned to fists, a song turned to a cry.

Remember? I played it for you that first afternoon we met, and then later played you. Or was it you who played me? The next morning I had to steal back to my place, locked out by a room-mate who thought I had gone on a bender, taken to the streets. Well I had, kind of. I swear I was intoxicated. I remember you were making cut-outs. Pictures from glossy magazines strewn all over, pinned to the walls. A head here, an arm there, legs and eyes, breasts and thighs, a neck lying in a heap of coloured light. (Or shall I call it delight?) What I do know for certain, if anything, is that for the moment we were still whole, my hand still connected to my heart, to yours, my touch still to brain and skin and laughter.

When I played you the song you thanked me and I confessed
I never thanked her for teaching it to me. And at that moment
I wished I had more than anything. But I was young and growing
fast and never thought much about the song or her, thinking
both far too tragic and old fashioned. Besides, the crunch of bone,
teeth, and eyes blooming like violets played their own song
that rode the wave of her life until the day she died. You loved
tragedies you said and asked me to play her one small cry, over
and over again, on a mattress on a floor, of a white room. As for
the cut-outs, you said they were a project in communication, as
you spread your limbs like a bird in flight. It was only later when
we got into one another and couldn't get out, found ourselves
pinned, and slapped and cried and sliced, until we too were strewn
all over, that I finally understood what the song meant, what release
she had been singing for. As I now come back to you, the bandages
long removed, the wounds but faint scars to sing.

## ADDRESS UNKNOWN

What do you do with words
you carefully weight,
put a price on,
that return empty?
Nine o'clock, and I listen
to traffic locked to pavement
swelling like a hot drug.
Watch a farmer's field growing
crows and gulls that appear
as if to confirm opposites attract,
then in another act
of confirmation,
disappear.

The last time you said all you wanted
was to make the hurt go away,
but it was too late.
You were wearing tight black
in the high noon sun
though you still looked chilled.
I thought of wrapping my arms
around you, but
I knew it wouldn't do any good.
Instead we spoke
of paths that narrow
to nothing.

As in the end, when there is nothing left
to do but wait. For these friends
I never see. And continue
to write even when there is no address.
As I now write to you
to say this may very well be the last time,
as each time often is.
No colourful postcard.
No letter.
Just these words
to wish you.

## MEDITATION

The sidewalk melts as if it were spring
but it's not, far from it,
I jump to avoid the splash.

A boy approaches who turns out not
to be a boy at all but a little old man.

There was a time I enjoyed puddles.

A young woman stares past, her eyes
tell me she's looking for someone.
I wonder if she knows who?

I pass myself in a glass-encased skyscraper.
The reflection reminds me of someone else.

The letters I write disappear
into the red mailbox at the corner
and out of my control.

Your response is distant and silent.
I picture you in a room sparsely furnished
the buzz of European traffic below.

You slit open my letters with a long thin blade.

Today I'll demand the garage attendant
makes certain he fixes the car properly.
Bitch. Bitch. Bitch.

What do they mean? I mean all these letters
I send and receive.

Cars are accidental, people are not. Both
honk and speed off in all directions.
My wet feet sneeze.

Even the noise is shredded by a moment
of sharp calm.

What would you do if one day I showed up
at your door (in place of a letter)
would we stop trying to understand?

This woman staring at me looked a lot like you.

My reflection confused me. For a moment it made me
feel old, then young.

They say the temperature is rising. Spring
has nothing to do with it.

No, I haven't been seeing anyone else.
Yes, I've thought of it.

When I arrive at the garage I know exactly what
I'll say. I have been rehearsing.

I was old and saw her as she was.
Then I was young and didn't see.
What would you say if you could see me now?

They say the car's a crime.

They constantly ask about you.
You have friends who know something I don't.

Some days pass as if I've slept through them.
Other days rant and rave.
Then there are the ones in between.

I still introduce you at parties.
Is love a fixation? Is loneliness?

I promise to keep walking after they repair the car.

I'll also continue to write even after you've returned
and everything is back to normal, or at least
normal as possible.

## BESSIE'S BLUES

*Whatever pathos there is in the world, whatever sadness she had,*
*was brought out in her singing.*
— Frank Schiffman, owner of Harlem's Lafayette theatre, Bluesland

I have always believed we are smaller than our words.
They carry us. Take on life. I spoke to you of this,
and you spoke of losing everything.

And up a flight of stairs into the music of Bessie Smith
(i ain't got nobody...),
you held my hands in welcome,
which I saw as her doing. Her words, her gift,
a heart-filled flutter, offering a brief reprieve
touch. You smiled and said you understood perfectly.

Though later you called me love, and I said, No,
it's the words (not wanting to sound foolish or vain),
their intimate beauty and sorrow. And me
wanting more than anything.

While all around you flames, tears
trying desperately to quench a smouldering ruin.
To extinguish a fire we must build a fire,
I said, and we saw evening turn scarlet
as we moved to the tip of it,
and into sheets
of morning.

Where you again said, Love.
And I said, Yes,
        because I like happy endings,
        wanted us to be happy,
        good for each other,
and you rose to dress, kissed me, and I whispered
into your ear
(Bessie, Bessie,
dear).

## PICTURE

a quiet rendezvous
     a cocktail lounge,
the band playing a soft
     "Night in Tunisia."
Your spine keys to her delicate touch,
     her neck the beginning of an oasis.
What you say is dripped
     onto skin,
blown into glass.

Owls perched side by side
     in a boreal city
don't say goodnight
     instead
swirl dark drinks
     the way of deserts
and balmy seas

The street is full on a Friday night
     snow the whites
of a million eyes
     everywhere.
Walking you don't kiss
     though continue to touch
now with talons
     hot as dry ice.

## LETTER

You are a memory dressed
in black, a shadow memory,
I want to reach for
and touch. So each day I wait
in sun-beaten clarity
and do not even attempt
to move into backyard shade.

Instead I choose the front steps,
sit while kids pound the pavement
screaming and swearing basketball,
listen to all these voices
saying nothing,
watch all this running
going nowhere.

True. I am waiting for your letter,
the response I've already rewritten
and mailed from what already
seems like years
ago. It frightens me
this memory,
how it can get so dark
and confused,
in such light.

## EASY

*Man found lying unconscious in bushes outside of apartment building.*
*— The Toronto Star*

It isn't easy to say I slammed into your room
more than once with gun in mind,
with metal claws sharp enough to tear
your clothes without touching you.
Do you believe it?
Is such a thing possible?
It isn't easy to admit
I could have killed
twisted and turned something numb
and dumb like myself from head to foot
having slipped in a crack in the street,
never landing but once,
the time I pushed my body into you
and saw a bead of water
suspended in a window
and tasted hot salt.

It isn't easy to say it was me who jumped
from that second floor
and landed in a bed of roses,
cut and fucked, my red dripping heart
pierced to the point of a shriek,
for me for me to say lust lust
no love love drove me off. And you
in shock, naked
in your stockings, no 911,
ambulance emergency, no nothing.
Well don't just stand there get me a drink,
I said, and you did, came down
and tilted my head back to the stars
that I swore were buttons

to a private place
I could only gasp for,
spiked to the ground.

It isn't easy to say, Ahh, those were the days
because they weren't,
they were nights
with you and me hemmed to a sheet
that pushed and pulled like an ocean
like the time I moved cities
and woke up to you
living across the street.
By accident, you said.
By gravity, or maybe static,
I said. Up a creaky flight of stairs
where I offered regret
blue and wet as our touch in a room
where a garden was growing on musty wallpaper.
It isn't easy to say, admit it
bet you never thought
living in a house with a fence and a husband
and children (how old are they now anyway?),
living without me,
could be so easy.

*The "union of irreconcilables": marriage of water and fire.*
– C. G. Jung, Dreams

It is not a matter of what to say.
That is all too easy.

> Regret 35, for example, has him
> standing under her window
> carrying on like a hyena.

But what not to say
so there is no confusion.
No need to point
and twist.

> Regret 90, finds them living in darkness
> for days loving carelessly.

It's not that they've tasted
all these passing years
with each other
still in their mouths.

> Regret 198, has their daily phone calls
> becoming nourishment.

It's not like that at all.
More it's a matter
of trying not to forget.
(at least the good parts)

> Regret 239, they are bleeding themselves dry
> of everyone and everything.

Holding the flame
they once were
Liquid fire in the palm of their hands

     Regret 300, believing there was no other
     way to live.

Blowing on it
from time to time
letting it burn deeply
if it must

     Regret 365, realizing goodbye
     was for good.

So that they might
keep in touch.

## TOMATO HEART

He gives her his heart
red as the autumn he left last week
in the east, before flying west,
when he lifted his canoe onto the water's rocky surface,
shifted his weight against the gunnels, and pushed off
into a sumptuous orgasm of colour.

Too much! he can already hear her say.
(Such hyperbole!)
This is a plum tomato not a heart,
and whoever heard of such a gift?

More likely she will say, too little.
Too little too late.
But this he gives her all the same.
It is all he has at hand,
for her to toss
to the birds
or put to taste.

## BEAR

A young woman crawls into his bed
warms it golden in the late afternoon.
He returns after a day's outing,
stealing honey, munching ants,
causing general ruckus.

Then, again, perhaps he's home from school.

He opens the door only to find her
scattered clothes
which he trails to her body.
She has come to be devoured.
Every morsel.

So he begins with toes, feet, moves to leg
up inside of thigh.
When he gets to the tenderest part,
she whimpers for him
to stop.

She is losing herself to his bare kiss.

But the moment he does, she whispers
to go on. And he does,
as though together
they were retelling
an old-time story.

## GERONIMO'S WATERMELONS

In New Mexico snow surprised us
the evening I was leaving.
She said it was a gift
for my journey,
beauty in a land
where the sky splits with meaning,
round and full like the melon he holds
in that famous photograph at Fort Sill.

His prison for life.

From Albuquerque head south on Highway 25,
and then swing west into last light,
the Gila mountains
his place of birth,
and you are there seventy years later.
When I got out of her car
I held out my palms as though to grasp
a handful of stars.

## SONG

I remember you well in the French café,
on the rainy day, you said you were leaving.
And without a sound, you turned around
and walked out into the city. Somewhere
in Montreal, I can't recall, but you
were dark and beautiful.

Marguerite, is that you I see again?
Marguerite, is that you on the street again?

Black crow sitting on a post,
laughing at us both, that's the way
the world turns. Trick in his eye
an old old song. All that's right
with us, and all that's wrong.

Marguerite, is that you I see again?
Marguerite, is that you on the street again?

I hold to the day you went away,
in the wind, in the rain, in my letters
that say, How do you do?
Are you through? Have you finally
found what you are looking for?

Marguerite, is that you I see again?
Marguerite, is that you on the street again?

Yes, I remember you well, on that day,
you turned and waved, oh so careless,
oh so brave. You said you'd placed
your bets, there were no regrets,
there was only life and everafter.

Marguerite, is that you I see again?
Marguerite, is that you on the street again?

## SHUT IN A ROOM

In the middle of a day
thick with longing
my only company
is a portrait by Klimt
(this is a tasteful room)
of a young woman in blue
which makes me wonder
if she took him
to her bed before
or after he painted her

And more, if her bones
long turned to dust
carried the memory
of all she felt
for him (that instant in 1902)
into the earth
along with the coming
rain

## It Happens

At first I see you in purple, cloak,
scarf and beret, moving from door
onto street remade by snow and light.
You turn briefly and wave.
And already I know this moment
is held only by us who have already moved past it,
through the beauty of its colour and absence,
        into the suddenness of spring
and you nearly naked lying near water
so silver I need to shield my eyes with my hand.
Again you turn and wave.

If I stopped this ritual we live through,
dream through, this very moment, here,
now, closed my eyes, clenched my fingers
into fists and held them still, where
would you be? Who would you be?
A stranger in a taxi speeding to an airport?
A lover opening a door and entering?
There is much I want to tell,
tell you that I am doing my best.
There is much I do not want to tell,
want you to discover for yourself.

But truth is I am doing what I can.
Each morning I feed the cat who lives indoors
along with the one who lives outdoors.
When it is cold one wants in.
When it is warm one wants out.
It's just the way it has been
for as long as I can remember.
Two lives. Two worlds.
When you return you will wave and
another season will greet me like a kiss.
And I will tell you I don't know which one of us
is going to outlast the other,
which one is here for long.

## EARTH POEM

Through it all
there is only you
I pretend to know.
Though I have known plenty.
Believed in more.

Many things go unsaid.
You ask for poetry
and I turn to a slim volume
of a visionary who dreamed
in solitude and searched all his life.

In the morning we go for breakfast
and the waitress smiles.
I wonder if she too has fled
through forest
only to turn and wait.

We have all been there
or want to be.
I breathe you in
your earthy woman smell.
Tell you I want to get so close
I don't want to shower you off.

## BLUEBERRIES

The end of summer
and we pick blue
berries, pluck them
with delicate precision,
    open ourselves to the goodness
    of the world
    that is theirs
drop the offering
onto our ready tongues
and drift into heavy clouds
bringing us to remember

friends who move
marry
make pies and jam
they ate as children for their own children,
holding to the sweetness
they once loved

and divorced
that's them too
when fingers cramp, stop,
mouths close in denial,
and the heart's want
is replaced by the sickly feeling
of having too much
too little.

But here kneeling in the ruins
of stumps as far as the eye can see,
we take these berries,
blue as the new life they are,
      in gratitude,
      humility,
      yet lustful for the taking.
The dusty logging road at our backs,
we stand, stretch to leave
at day's end
and laugh in our full desire
all the way home.

"*Geronimo and Apache Sitting Beside Train.*"
— *courtesy the Smithsonian Institute*

# DANCE *to* HOLD ON

## DANCE TO HOLD ON

Dance to hold on
to who you are.

It's what you do
with half your life in prison.

You dance
the distant land
of your Apache home.

And become a show
a curious spectacle
for the city folks
who come to see
authentic savage custom.

What they do not see is your spirit
dance to hold on.

You who will later
try to convince
your people,
yourself,
you are better off
to forget.

He's already asleep when he awakes to someone rapping
the back door. The sound thunders through the small house
and so he creeps up out of bed and into the kitchen.

But his mother is already there in the dimly lit room peeking
through the window in the door before opening it and uttering
a short cry.

Then, almost instantaneously, she hears him and returns to her
adult self as she turns and snaps at him to get back to bed.

He wilts before her fierce look but not before almost seeing
who it is. He doesn't return to bed but sits in the shadows and
peers through the dark hallway.

In the kitchen the noise of a porcelain wash-pan being filled
and cloth ripped and soaked as he tries to understand what
is going on.

Although their words are hushed, the boy can hear his mother
ask what happened, then curse (Jesus Christ Almighty!),
between slurred sobs that make his heart pound.

He now knows who she is, and he hears her try to answer,
give some reason why she got beat up, make it sound like
an accident.

## DOMINATION

How many hurts does it take
before you can hear yourself?
Count the pieces that talk back
in the heart's red mirror.
Nerve quilt, flesh infused
with blood pricks and acid memory.

How many hurts does it take!
she pleads, slamming the bottle down.
One too many, two too many,
three too many, four....
   "Why?" She asks (again & again).
   "Why did you do it?"

This is pain. Not the sensation but the person.
She is pain. Pained. Racked.
Little voice, needle voices, sizzling voices
vying for domination, back there
tunnelled through brain, skin and time.
Back, far back, when it, that thing, happened.
   "Mother!... Why?... Father?"

Out of its shell a chick pokes a head
that is bit off - forever.
But tonight she acts,
throws her glass against the wall.
This woman. Lovely woman.
Shattered woman.

# SURPRISE

Tonight there is the dream of family in jail, not seen in years, dead. The one who pries open the door of a neighbour's house and takes a seat at the kitchen table, goes about preparing himself a midnight feast of toast and jam. Smiles to the owners when they creep down to investigate, asks them to join him in good trickster fashion. Thinks nothing of it, as if in the home of the good Samaritan he could do no wrong.

I was hungry, he confesses to a judge who promptly locks him up.

A painter who doesn't paint. He calls and off we go to see a film on Munch, and he is caught in the blue silence, knowing it intimately as his own, a mouth filled with mute pain. The next day he asks me to bring over a bottle of sweet wine (something the bees would like) for his parole officer, who has traded her uniform for her nakedness. I knock lightly, and he comes to the door belly hard, and we clasp hands in the hallway and laugh out loud.

I turn to leave without wondering if I will ever see him again.

The dream of him visiting that one summer still alive in its smallness, knowing he had nowhere else to go. Fifteen and shoeless (mom gave him a pair of dad's), he catches a freight train north to us hoping to stay but doesn't, can't. Poverty too good a fit for us all. He swears he'll come back and beats up the local bully before leaving (don't fuck with family) and highballs it to Toronto, where he waits for a hand that comes too late to mean what it should. And begins to die, in and out of jail, in and out of himself, so that even his new bride with all her beauty and love cannot save him. So that even his death in a downtown rooming house, its bitter sadness, comes as no surprise.

## The Fallen

Back then you just didn't give a damn.
Young strength does that.
Lets you play loose
as a warrior, gives you the power,
let's you take it
as it comes. Puke,
laugh and start over.
From poolroom to party,
close the bar every night.
Then onto the street stone-frozen
looking for more. Or maybe
someone to be more.

I still remember him in the toilet
washing down a handful of acid
with a bottle of Southern Comfort.
And to think I had just gone in for a leak.
What else to do
in those days?
Walk for hours
counting blinding snowflakes
to avoid the scene at home,
avoid yourself. Wait
for a hand
that never comes.

Years later in the Sault,
flown in to sound literary,
a community worker asks me if I knew him.
Fried himself.
Created his own cosmology, a world
of gods and demons battling it out
in his head. Lived on the street,
got so people were afraid of him.
Guess he realized
what he'd become.
Jumped,
just last week from a high-rise.
And still with no one
to catch him.

# FOR THE WOMAN WHO FELL FROM THE SKY

*WOMAN FALLS FROM SKY. Miami — A woman who fell from the sky died after hitting a garden wall in an apartment complex yesterday. Police have no idea who she is or where she came from.* — The Associated Press

Torso twisted by gravity,
body flattened
at thirty-two feet per second
against cement
with a deadened
bone-crunching thud.
A crowd gathered
and looked up. Just in case.
Police whispered. Sirens roared.
Ambulance attendants wondered
what they should do.

Where could this unidentified
woman have come from?
Did she fall from a building?
Her broken condition
showed she must have
fallen from much higher.
Did she jump from a plane?
This nameless woman
perhaps pushed.
What other explanation?

Except to conjure an old story,
old as the land itself,
of a woman who fell in love
with the handsome stars
and cast herself to live among them,
until one dancing evening
she slipped and fell
through a hole in the sky
but unlike this one,
bent and broken,
landed safely
in a softer time.

## In Silence

You laugh, and I look into your dark eyes
and know there is a hurt, a swell,
a bruise (what can I call it?) rawer
than most can imagine.
I see it more a delicate orchid,
blood tender
something that stirs, grows, pulses,
that you keep hidden in the folds of your flesh,
camouflaged by push-up bra, blouse, skin-tight jeans.

This very moment I see your lips pursed open,
head tilted back, hand casually playing with your hair,
mouth making sounds of casual conversation.
(Fuck this. Fuck that. Hey, long time no see.)
Until I whisper in your ear, I am sorry,
truly, about the accident,
your child,
and you look away
in silence.

My brother refuses to watch
it. He says it hurts too much
to see
how Geronimo's people
were treated.
>    It's only a movie,
>    I almost say,
>    but don't.
The reason
clear as the good water we drink
by just looking at the kids at his knee.
Refugees
from other reserves
finding a home
in his heart.

# Logging Camp Photograph

*In the late 1800s saws replaced axes in the logging industry. By 1902,*
*an estimated 150 million trees had been cut and floated down the upper*
*Ottawa River system. — The Ottawa Citizen*

What you don't see is what interests you.

How they wake in darkness,
slide into frozen bodies,
hitch snorting horses,
hone shimmering blades,
swallow blister, toothache, backache,
amputate memory.
All winter burrowed

in their own stink, walls
of socks and underwear
strung under a ceiling they can touch,
over a fire with a mouth like hell
or heaven because outside
hands are fingerless clubs,
breath solid as the branches they skive off.

Come spring rivers overflow with mud
so thick horses sink,
they emerge grizzled
and bent. Nobody stays young for long.
Some will guide great log booms
down to the mill. Others
will take the money and clear out.
All will flee the ruin.

But this you don't see either.

## MISSING

A face held in the hands of a clock.
A wanted poster.
Not from the Old West,
imaginary Outlaws and Indians,
but on this street,
a child gone missing.

And somewhere a mother
chews her fingernails to flesh,
until her moons are no more.
No moon. No sun.
No night. No day.
Only the between of loss.

And my own mother warning my sister
to watch Him. Screaming
after we've returned from the store
with clothes and shoes,
a bow and arrow set for me.
And my sister screaming back
because she needs something to wear,
because she is tired of poverty
hounding her.

Until one day she too disappears
from her mother's grip
never to return,
to raise her own children
(she thinks)
differently.

## DIALOGUE

*(A response to Sujata Bhatt's "New World Dialogues.")*

What happens when journey
leads to a chasm wide as the Grand Canyon?
When you gave me your poem
you asked me to understand
what you were trying to do,
you were not the colonizer,
that you did not choose
these names,
they chose you:

Sun in the Pupil
Red Shirt Girl
Has a Dog
Spotted Thunder
Cast Away and Run
Wounded in Winter
Shedding Bear
Shake the Bird
Bring Earth to Her

"Burial of the Dead at the Battle of Wounded Knee. S.D."
(Copyrighted, Jan. 1st, 1891, and hung in a museum in
Germany.)

Has it come to this? you asked.
And I said (later), no, it is still going on.
That maybe it comes down to the young man
I met that earth-frozen December
high up at Acoma Pueblo in New Mexico,
huddled in his leather jacket
selling his family's pottery,
explaining their tradition
of generations,
and, in the same breath,
he was joining
the US Army.

## WHAT MATTERS YOU SAY

We go shopping for the past
and I imagine seeing you
on the street where
you were last strung out.
You could be anyone
but today you are
dear to me.

She gives me explanations,
the history of colonialism
the economic system
that corporate capitalism
has taken over the world
unemployment
sweatshop poverty.

I stop her in mid stride
and tell her you are
at it again. So young,
so messed up,
drunk on remorse
children never seen
parents
family
land
the whole kettle of worms.

# GERONIMO THE OLD MAN

His biographer Barrett is surprised not to find the painted warrior, hand twitching to cut his throat. Instead he finds an old man rocking his grandchild on his knee. Five-feet-nine in moccasins, wearing a blue suit and a red scarf, square shoulders, powerful, built like a man who has had to fight or flee nearly all his life.

What Barrett extracts from Geronimo goes deep behind the daring. The wizened face takes him to loss. The miles marked with graves through the killing years. Wives. Children. His own mother, strewn along a blood trail from New Mexico to Arizona to Old Mexico. And later in captivity, the disease: two more wives, one by one the children: Chappo in Alabama, Fenton and Lulu at Fort Sill, her own family, and then his last hope, Thomas, dead at eighteen, at Carlisle, the death camp for Indian students.

A basket of pollen, an eagle feather, an abalone shell, tobacco. You pray to Usen. Sing until the evening star is halfway between horizon and zenith. Sing for the Power. Sing for the strength not to turn away from your dead family. Sing to learn to pray to the God on the cross. To believe white people love you.

# THE ART OF SURVIVAL

The street swells with night
like a birth you don't want.
Is it the city again
getting under your skin?
You who were taught the art of survival.
Indian time, she said,
means scrubbing floors
at six.

Beads of blue light string the houses,
lock them to sitcom fantasy.
You think of joining in,
tuning out, almost do,
with a touch of the remote,
but the earth shifts and the cat turns
from its dish to prowl the floor,
looking for signs
of life.

At the darkened window a field
moves just beyond sight
and sound. Soon it will braid your dreams
and you will look ahead
to the past. This you know
just as you know tonight
the curved web of the dreamcatcher
will remain empty.

The cat paws the door to get out and hunt.
In the morning it will drag in a bird
or mouse and offer it to you
to eat. And you
having journeyed to the end
of sleep will see this
as an omen
of things to come.

## POSTSCRIPT

The train rattles across desert, and I find myself following you on a map written on my tongue. Dust and hot wind blowing into your face, the train roaring and belching smoke, and I am looking out of my second floor window, past the barren maple trees, beyond the faint autumn sun, looking to you and wondering what it's all about? This journey. For unlike in the before-time when your people fought and earned the name Apache, I see you chained, wrists and ankles, sweating in dismay, swallowed by the beast of progress winding its way towards doom.

I survey the high-rises and taste the word defeat on the edge of the 21st century.

Dream in the half-light of the Long Knives who hold you and have no comprehension who you are. Who they are. Where they are. On this land they are bent on speeding through. I want to tell them that the day will come when you will swallow them in the power of myth and the beauty of a galloping horse. In a power that will take their weapons and bend them like willow, change confinement to freedom, iron to feather. I want to tell them but I cannot. For I too am shut in. Today behind a glass. Tomorrow?

They say when you die you meet your fear.

This while you sit like rock, stare straight through these invaders from another world, keeping vigil over your people, who some say would be better off without you. Point the blame. This while you pray they are wrong, and the train arrives in the hot damp of Florida, and you are sentenced to hard labour for two years. Alabama for five. This is what I see when General Miles speaks of the terms of your surrender with a mouthful of promises dripping like sweet water, and you become prisoner of men who try to turn you into one of them. American.

The United States of America. Stolen land, you say.

And me, here in Canada, looking out on this heavy new millennium, seeing you seeing them. Wondering why? Why you? Why me? This journey? When the leaves are off the trees, holding the ground for winter, and I am on my padded chair, fingers to keys, and you on a hard bench, holding on for dear life. No camera at this moment, just cold blue eyes everywhere, watching your every gesture, ready to kill something they have already lost. The moment collapses and folds into now, and choice is bound to loss, of all that might have been.

It is too easy to become lost in the self. Is that what you are trying to say?

The Sergeant shrugs and spits a gob of tobacco juice on the floor. He grins, and I know he cannot begin to know your need to go home to your land, because for him you have no land. This is the new world. The new uninhabited world. You are a prisoner, and he is simply carrying out his order to transport you. Besides you are different, dangerous, and he firmly believes, given half the chance, you would run your knife under the skin of his scalp, clutch a clump of hair and pull. This before he would even have time to point his gun, let alone fire. He hears himself calling for help.

"Jesus, merciful father!" It is a terrible thing this fear.

It swells inside until that's all there is, and all he sees is blood red. It comes to this, and I don't want to be here any longer. I go outside for air, kick through leaves that the wind takes like birds. Back inside, I am perched on the roof of the train hauling you away. It has stopped to take on water for the boiler. You are sitting with your few warriors in the prairie grass growing along the edge of the tracks. You are a celebrity. A photographer sets up his box camera and takes your picture. "Smile," he says, without thinking. And I wonder if it is really you? Some say the one we see in the photographs is merely an impersonator? Someone designated to lead away from the real trail.

Will the real Geronimo please smile.

One thing for certain: your spirit, this thing we never see, exists on the land, in the hills, grass, rock, soil, in the air itself. I breathe deep and wonder how long before the paved drive-by culture of America strips the last remnants of you off the land. Yesterday the newspaper had an article about a space station under construction. Space, the final frontier. The cliché sets off an alarm because it sounds like what they said about the Old West a hundred years ago. Sounds like murder and displacement. What makes them think it would be any different next time around? History shows otherwise. Again, I see your people fenced in under the hard labour of stone and iron.

They hunt you for your old beliefs.

The rules say that from now on you are to live under the white man's law. If you do not give yourself up to reservation life, sell your people to a life of stagnation and poverty, all the power of the United States of America will be unleashed upon you, and you will be hunted down. They warn you that its terrible ferocity will tear you to pieces. You pray to Usen but to no avail. No wind comes to blow these whitemen back into the great water. Their kind of power is too new and treacherous. Their Iron Serpent continues to roar over your homeland. Until finally even you are inside it. Some of your few kill themselves in despair. Jump from cliffs. Slit their throat.

It is what you get for not obeying the rules.

Later, as prisoner of war, you confront Wratton, the Superintendent of Indians, who sells your cattle (the few you are allowed to raise) and keeps the money. While your people go hungry. He shouts he doesn't care what you say. You are nothing. Your power is gone. You can do nothing to stop the greed, which has now become the American way. At this moment, your young Apache helper jumps him and manages to stab him with a homemade knife. The cut is superficial, merely muscle and fat, and Wratton recovers to have him beaten and thrown into prison. It is the young who will take over. You feel it in your bones. But to what end?

Days become an age of miracles: electricity, combustion, refrigeration, nuclear power, microchips.

There is a famous photograph of you in old age in your melon patch with your children beside you, a simple pleasure. Behind you the world is going by. And I am made to think of the Aboriginal Career Symposium I attended, watching all the young people mulling over their options, their future beckoning them like a promise. And I wondered how they will maintain their identity and survive in a society whose advertising slogan is a way of life. That tells them to consume and be like everyone else. Outside, on the telephone-computer lines, a blackbird caws to tell me we are still here. What would you say? If you saw your people now.

The statistics show few Indigenous languages will survive the 21st century.

The bird takes off, and a chill runs through me in the cold dawn. The wise say that to be leader, one must know humility above all. Everyone must come before one's own interest. Every interest must be balanced against another. Geronimo, I hear your laughter when I say this aloud. "Show me the one," I dream you say. The sun rises brilliant, tobacco is down, and once again it is time to go indoors. Choices. Decisions. To remain passive or to act. Adapt or die. Why you chose to escape the grinding reservation poverty, the threats, I can understand. Why you killed to defend your people and the old way of life that too I can understand. And I can even understand the American soldiers whose job it was to capture you in the name of their civilization. It's the deceit and greed that boggles the mind.

Even in your whiteman's clothes, you stand for your beliefs.

From your surrender in 1886 until your death in 1909, despite your pathetic pleas for the USA to honour the terms of the treaty, your Bedonkohe never again saw their homeland. Instead you are invited by Roosevelt himself to take part in his Presidential inauguration. As though that would be enough. How much does it take to break a spirit? A friend calls and asks me what I am doing. I say your name, Geronimo. And I am greeted by silence. How to respond to such a name? A name kids and soldiers use to jump from swings or planes. A name that passes through time and place. From the desert of the southwest USA up to Canada to a tree-lined street. I think of your red earth and mention a trip to your grave.

I could say I was drawn to you.

Instead we talk about the Free Leonard Peltier rally this coming Sunday on Parliament Hill. For twenty-five years an American Indian Prisoner of War in the USA. She tells me about a recent article by a prominent Canadian journalist, comparing Peltier to Mandela. And I add Geronimo. Fort Sill. Leavenworth. It's all the same. Before hanging up, I tell her to dress warm, I expect Sunday to be dark and cold to mark the occasion. And that's it. The day now in full swing, slam of neighbours and traffic breaking through the walls. A local radio station announces the news of the day and fittingly neglects to mention the rally. Life going on in all directions, or not going on, freedom or confinement, sky or ceiling.

## ACKNOWLEDGEMENTS

A special thanks to Judith and to family and friends whose presence has given me much of whatever I may write. I would like to thank Coteau Books for their continued support, and Patrick Lane for his editorial acuity and generous encouragement, not only to me but to so many other younger writers. A chi-meegwetch also goes out to the community of writers and visual artists I have met over the years too numerous to mention by name – though I will mention names like the Banff Centre, En'owkin Centre and Returning The Gift – whose work continues to provide inspiration and moral support. Finally, an acknowledgement goes to The Canada Council for the Arts for providing support for another project which also afforded me time to work on this book.

Versions of the poems have appeared in the following journals and anthologies: ABSINTHE; *Anthology of Native Poetry in Canada* (broadview press); ASAIL (Assocation for Studies in American Indian Literature); *Canadian Literature* (University of British Columbia); *Event; Exposed: Aesthetics of Aboriginal Erotic Art* (MacKenzie Gallery); *Gatherings* (Theytus Books); *Meltwater: Fiction and Poetry From The Banff Centre for the Arts* (The Banff Centre Press); *Prairie Fire; Rampike; Red Earth* (University of Arizona); *The Windsor Review* (University of Windsor).

Much of the historical information on the life of Geronimo was found in *Geronimo, His Own Story,* as told to S. M. Barrett and *Geronimo: The Man, His Time* by Angie Debo. Other valuable sources about Geronimo and the Apache people include *They Moved like the Wind: Cochise, Geronimo and the Apache Wars* by David Roberts and *An Apache Life-Way* by Morris E. Opler. The landscape of the American southwest, which included a visit to the gravesite of Geronimo in Oklahoma, provided the initial impetus for the writing; then came the signs, the markers, that I continued to encounter in my travels – like postcards of Geronimo in Brighton and further references in Zurich and Tokyo – which compelled me to continue with this project. Unforeseen by me at the time, they drew present and past together, made the connections, and did much to determine the shape of this book.

## ABOUT THE AUTHOR

**ARMAND GARNET RUFFO'S** creative biography *Grey Owl: The Mystery of Archie Belaney* was published by Coteau Books in 1997. He has published another poetry collection, *Opening In the Sky*, and had professional productions of a playscript, *A Windigo Tale*. He has had poetry, fiction and essays appear in journals and anthologies both in Canada and abroad.

Armand Ruffo's work is strongly influenced by his Ojibway heritage. Born in Chapleau, in northern Ontario, he now lives in Ottawa, where he teaches in the Department of English Language and Literature at Carleton University.